LANGUAGE ARTS

Learning About

Fiction

by Martha E. H. Rustad

Consulting Editor: Gail Saunders-Smith, PhD
Consultant: Kelly Boswell, educational consultant

CAPSTONE PRESS
a capstone imprint

Pebble Plus is published by Capstone Press,
1710 Roe Crest Drive, North Mankato, Minnesota 56003
www.capstonepub.com

Library of Congress Cataloging-in-Publication Data
Rustad, Martha E. H. (Martha Elizabeth Hillman), 1975–
 Learning about fiction / Martha E. H. Rustad.
     pages cm.—(Language arts)
 Includes bibliographical references and index.
 ISBN 978-1-4914-0578-9 (hb)—ISBN 978-1-4914-0612-0 (eb)—ISBN 978-1-4914-0646-5 (pb)
 1. Fiction—Authorship—Juvenile literature. 2. Creative writing—Juvenile literature. I. Title.
 PN3355.R87 2014
 808.3—dc23   2014001855

Editorial Credits
Erika L. Shores, editor; Terri Poburka, designer; Charmaine Whitman, production specialist

Photo Credits
Capstone Studio: Karon Dubke, 5, 7, 21; Capstone Illustrations: Cori Doerrfeld, cover, 7, 9, 11, 13, 15, 17, 19; Shutterstock: Gelpi JM, cover

Design Elements
Shutterstock: Lisovskaya Natalia

For Kirsten.—MEHR

Note to Parents and Teachers

The Language Arts set supports Common Core State Standards for Language Arts related to craft and structure, to text types and writing purpose, and to research for building and presenting knowledge. This book describes and illustrates fiction. The images support early readers in understanding the text. The repetition of words and phrases helps early readers learn new words. This book also introduces early readers to subject-specific vocabulary words, which are defined in the Glossary section. Early readers may need assistance to read some words and to use the Table of Contents, Glossary, Read More, Internet Sites, Critical Thinking Using the Common Core, and Index sections of the book.

Printed in the United States of America in North Mankato, Minnesota.
032014   008087CGF14

Table of Contents

Let's Read

Grab a book. Let's read!

Is your book about a dog

that cooks? Or maybe it's about

a girl who flies. Fiction books

tell made-up stories.

The author is the person who has a story idea and writes it down. An illustrator draws pictures to help tell the story.

author

illustrator

Characters

In a story, characters talk and act.

Let's read a story about a lost dog.

Anna and Henry are characters

in the story.

One morning my brother Henry and I were walking to school.

"Hey, Anna, that dog is following us!" Henry said.

"I think she's lost," I said.

"What do we do?" Henry said. "I know! Let's take her to school with us!"

Anna is the story's narrator.

A narrator tells the story.

Dialogue is the words characters

say to each other. Dialogue is

surrounded by quotation marks.

"Dogs can't go to school!" I said to Henry.

"We can't just leave her here," Henry said.

"Let's ask Mr. Hill for help," I said.

Setting

The setting is where the story takes place. Anna and Henry are outside Forestview School.

Mr. Hill, the principal of Forestview School, walked toward us.

"Good morning, Anna and Henry," Mr. Hill said. "Is this your dog?"

"No. We think she is lost," Henry said.

The setting also tells when

a story takes place. This story

happens in the morning,

before school.

It was almost time for the bell to ring.

"What should we do, Mr. Hill?" I asked.

"Let's check her collar," Mr. Hill said. "Owners sometimes put
a phone number on their dog's tags."

Plot

What happens in a story is called the plot. Characters sometimes solve a problem. Henry and Anna want to find the lost dog's owner.

"But Mr. Hill, this dog's collar is missing!" Henry said.

"Poor dog," I said. "How will we ever find her owners?"

A story has a beginning,
a middle, and an end.
How does the story about
the lost dog end?

Henry's teacher Mrs. Lewis walked toward us.

"Oh my!" she said. "How did Rosie get here?"

"This is your dog?" I said.

Just then the bell rang.

"I don't have time to take Rosie home," Mrs. Lewis said.
"Can she join my class, Mr. Hill?"

"I think that would be OK," answered Mr. Hill.

"Cool!" Henry said. "Now Rosie really will go to school with me!"

Kinds of Fiction

What is your favorite

kind of fiction?

A storybook? A mystery?

Read some fiction today!

Glossary

author—someone who writes books

character—a person or animal in a story

dialogue—words spoken out loud by characters in a story

fiction—a made-up story

illustrator—someone who draws pictures

narrator—a character that tells the story

plot—what happens in a story

quotation marks—punctuation marks around words said out loud

setting—the place and time of a story

Read More

Ganeri, Anita. *Funny Stories.* Writing Stories. Chicago: Heinemann Library, 2013.

Manushkin, Fran. *What Happens Next, Katie?: Writing a Narrative with Katie Woo.* Katie Woo, Star Writer. North Mankato, Minn.: Picture Window Books, 2014.

Rustad, Martha E. H. *The Parts of a Book.* Wonderful World of Reading. North Mankato, Minn.: Capstone Press, 2013.

Internet Sites

FactHound offers a safe, fun way to find Internet sites related to this book. All of the sites on FactHound have been researched by our staff.

Here's all you do:

Visit *www.facthound.com*

Type in this code: 9781491405789

Check out projects, games and lots more at **www.capstonekids.com**

Critical Thinking Using the Common Core

1. Dialogue is the words spoken out loud by characters in a story. Give an example of dialogue from page 19. (Craft and Structure)

2. What are the three main parts of a fiction story? (Key Ideas and Details)

Index

Word Count: 187 (main text)
Grade: 1
Early-Intervention Level: 14